MW01533508

DISCARD
DISCARD

Abraham Lincoln

Jennifer Strand

abdopublishing.com

Published by Abdo Zoom™, PO Box 398166, Minneapolis, Minnesota 55439. Copyright © 2017 by Abdo Consulting Group, Inc. International copyrights reserved in all countries. No part of this book may be reproduced in any form without written permission from the publisher. Abdo Zoom™ is a trademark and logo of Abdo Consulting Group, Inc.

Printed in the United States of America, North Mankato, Minnesota
072016
092016

THIS BOOK CONTAINS RECYCLED MATERIALS

Cover Photo: Alexander Gardner/Library of Congress
Interior Photos: Alexander Gardner/Library of Congress, 1, 4; Everett Historical/Shutterstock Images, 5; Nancy Carter/North Wind Picture Archives, 6; North Wind Picture Archives, 7, 18–19; Mathew B. Brady/Library of Congress, 8; Gregory Horne/iStockphoto, 8–9; AP Images, 10–11; Anthony Berger/Library of Congress, 12; Hulton Archive/iStockphoto, 13; George Peter Alexander Healy, 15; A. Brett & Co./Library of Congress, 16

Editor: Brienna Rossiter
Series Designer: Madeline Berger
Art Direction: Dorothy Toth

Publisher's Cataloging-in-Publication Data
Names: Strand, Jennifer, author.
Title: Abraham Lincoln / by Jennifer Strand.
Description: Minneapolis, MN : Abdo Zoom, [2017] | Series: Legendary leaders
    | Includes bibliographical references and index.
Identifiers: LCCN 2016941395 | ISBN 9781680792348 (lib. bdg.) |
    ISBN 9781680794021 (ebook) | 9781680794915 (Read-to-me ebook)
Subjects: LCSH: Lincoln, Abraham, 1809-1865--Political and social views--
    Juvenile literature. | Slaves--Emancipation--United States--Juvenile
    literature. | Antislavery movements--United States--History--19th century--
    Juvenile literature. | Presidents--United States--Biography--Juvenile
    literature. | Abolitionists--United States--Biography--Juvenile literature.
Classification: DDC 973.7092 [B]--dc23
LC record available at http://lccn.loc.gov/2016941395

Table of Contents

Abraham Lincoln was the 16th US president.

He led the country through the American Civil War (1861–1865).

Early Life

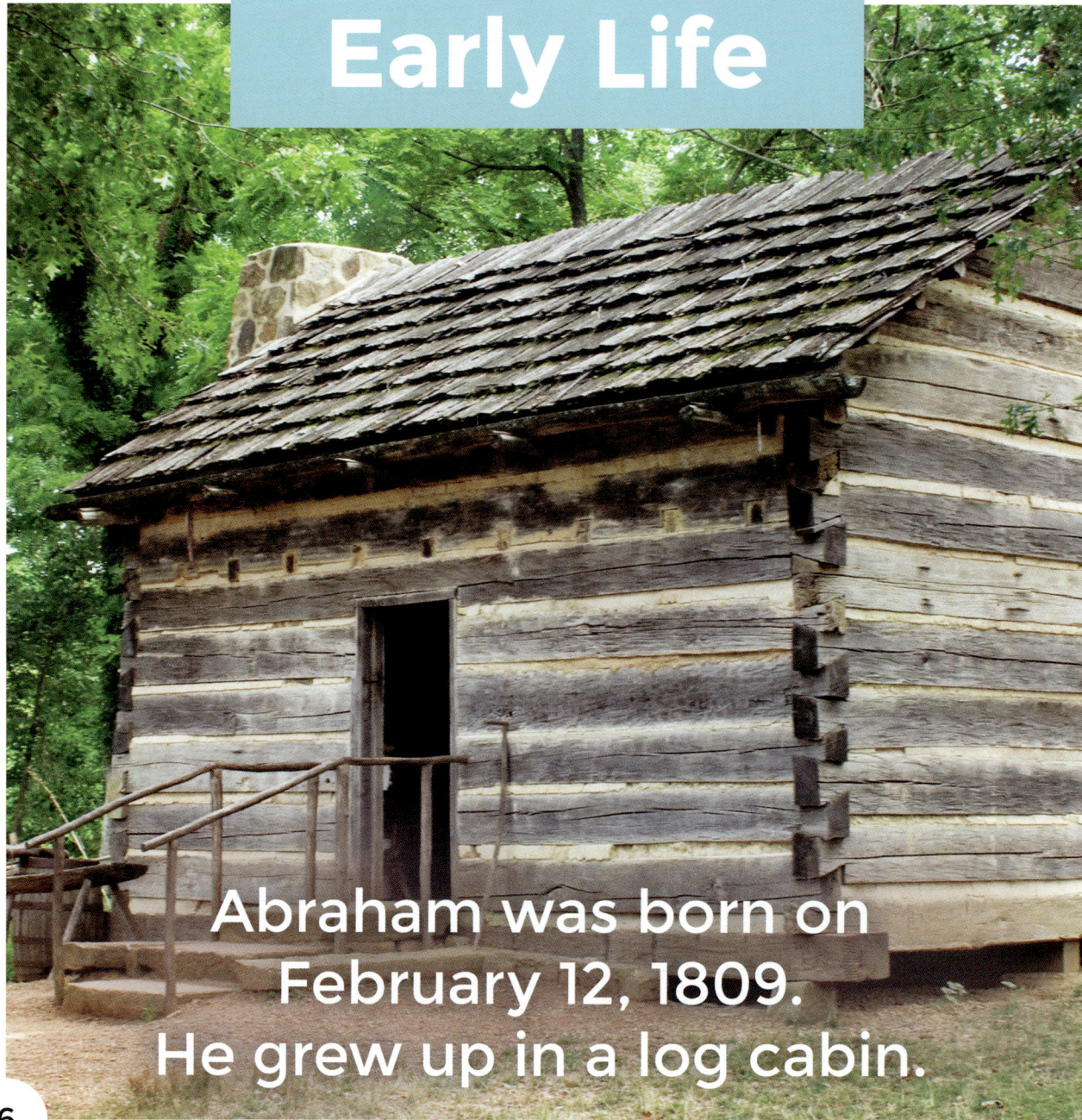

Abraham was born on
February 12, 1809.
He grew up in a log cabin.

His family was poor.
He could not always go to school.
But he loved to read.

Leader

Lincoln lived in Illinois.
He worked as a **lawyer**.
Later he became a **lawmaker**.
He was known for being honest.

Some states had **slavery**. Lincoln thought slavery was wrong. He spoke against it.

He took part in
many **debates**.

In 1861 Lincoln became president.

Some Southern states tried
to start a new country.
The American Civil War broke out.

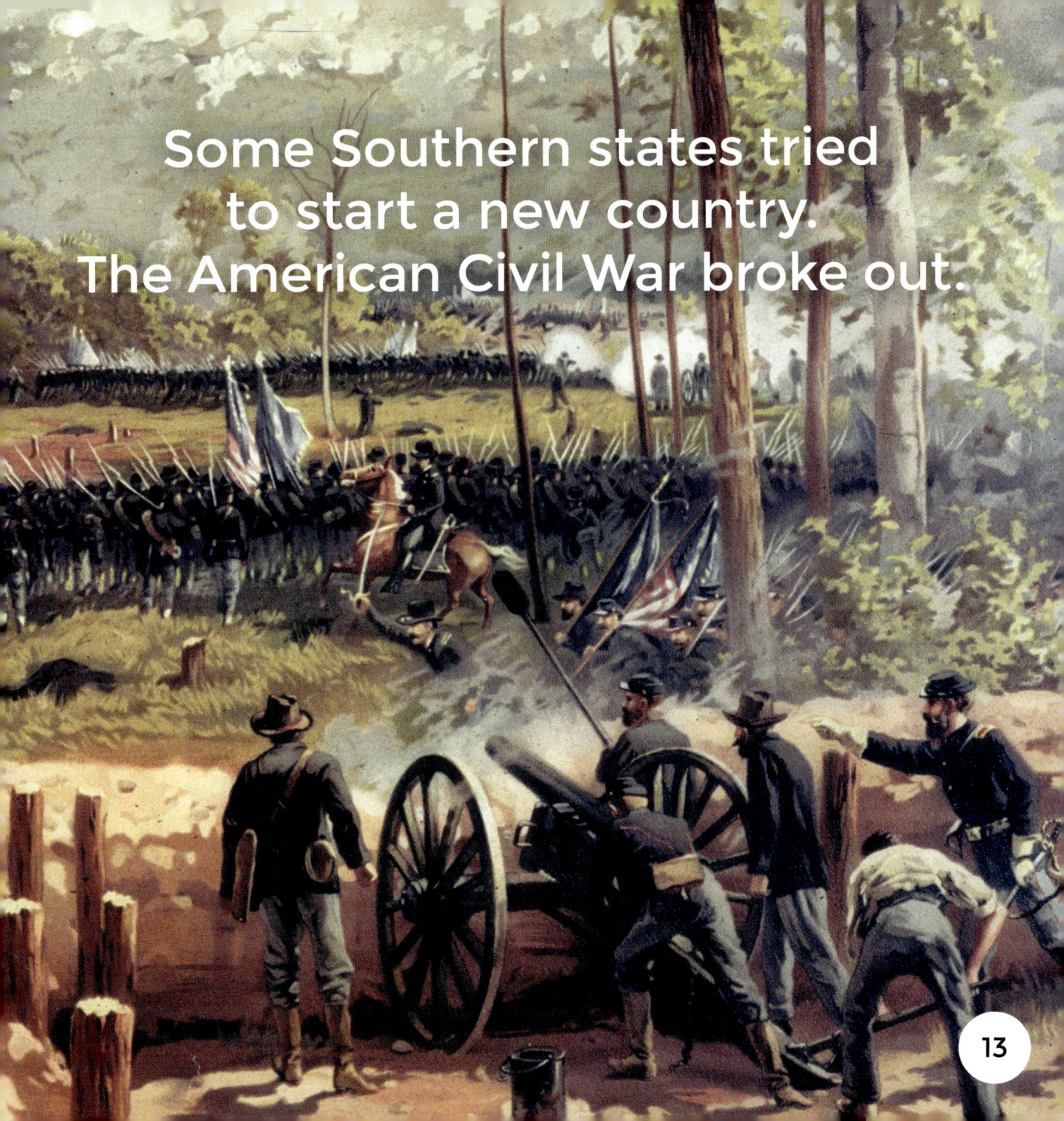

Lincoln tried to keep the country together. He also wanted to end slavery. In 1863 he said that slaves in the Southern states were free.

This made some
people angry.

15

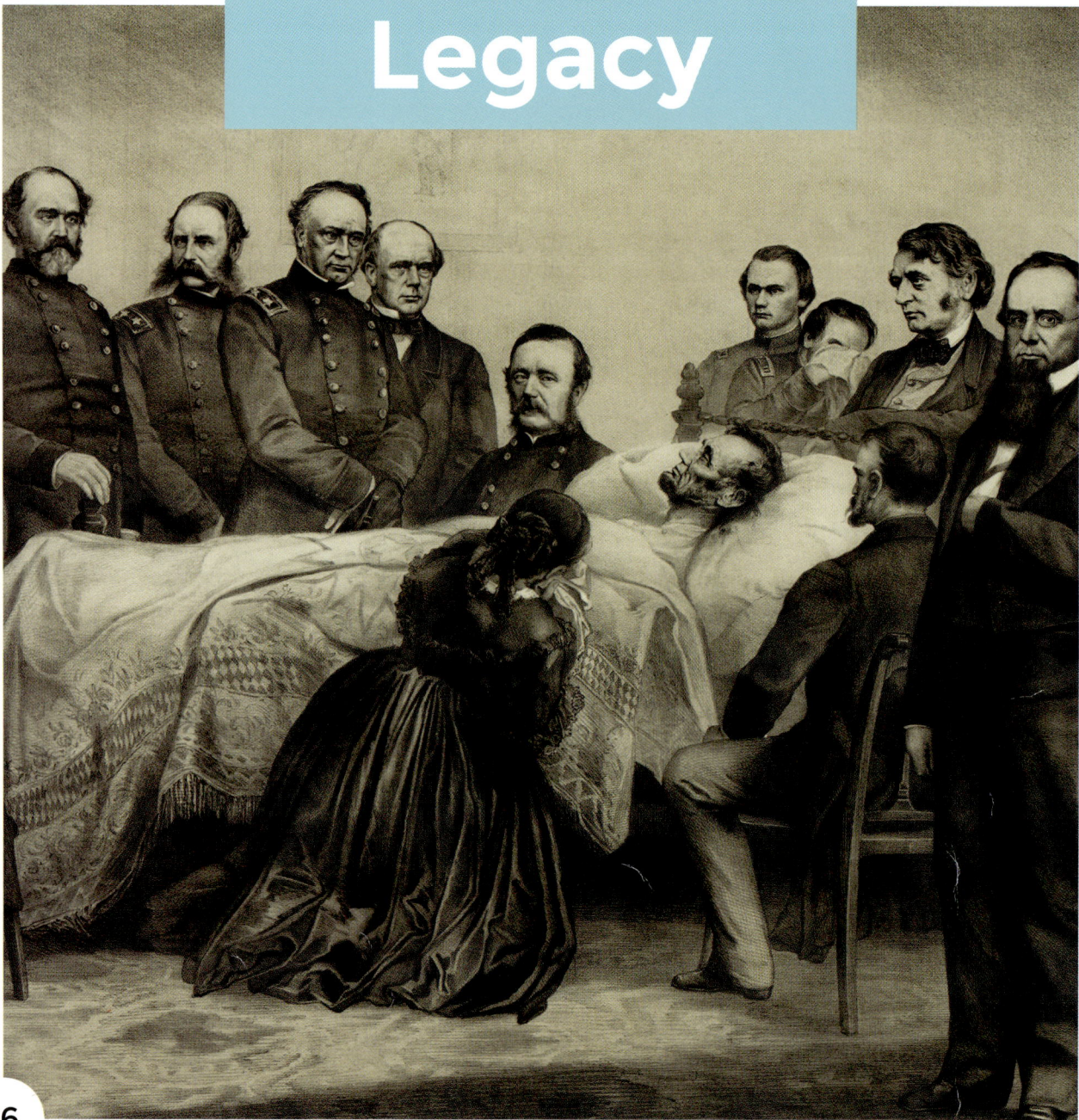

Legacy

Lincoln was shot on April 14, 1865. He died one day later. Soon after, the American Civil War ended.

Lincoln helped the country stay together. Many people believe he was one of the best presidents.

Abraham Lincoln

Born: February 12, 1809

Birthplace: Hodgenville, Kentucky

Known For: Lincoln was the 16th US president. He led the country during the American Civil War. He also worked to end slavery.

Died: April 15, 1865

Key Dates

1809: Abraham Lincoln is born on February 12.

1846: Lincoln is elected to Congress.

1861–1865: Lincoln is the US president.

1861–1865: The American Civil War is fought.

1863: Lincoln signs the Emancipation Proclamation.

1865: Lincoln is shot on April 14. He dies on April 15.

Glossary

debate - when two people talk in public about an idea or question.

lawmaker - a person who makes laws.

lawyer - a person who helps others in matters related to the law.

slavery - the practice of buying and owning other people against their will.

Booklinks

For more information
on **Abraham Lincoln**, please visit
booklinks.abdopublishing.com

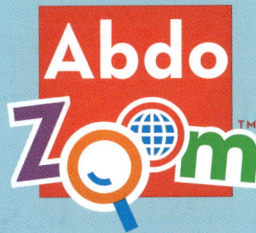

Abdo Zoom™

Zoom™ **In on Biographies!**

Learn even more with the Abdo Zoom
Biographies database. Check out
abdozoom.com for more information.

Index

American Civil War, 5, 13, 17

born, 6

debates, 11
died, 17

Illinois, 9

lawmaker, 9
lawyer, 9

president, 4, 12, 18

shot, 17
slavery, 10, 14
Southern states, 13, 14

DISCARD